Bucket Filling from A to Z

The Key to Being Happy

By Carol McCloud and Caryn Butzke

Illustrated by Glenn Zimmer

Bucket Fillosophy®

All around the whole, wide world in every city and town
you'll find happy boys and girls if you only look around.
They are called "Bucket Fillers." They fill buckets every day
with the good things that they do and the kind words that they say.

Everyone has a bucket that's invisible to the eye.
When it's full, you feel happy. When it's empty, you might cry.
The key to being happy is in this choice you make . . .
Will you fill a bucket or be mean and dip and take?

Bucket filling is easy, as easy as can be.
You can fill a bucket all the way from A to Z.
Here are some ideas for things that you can do
to make others happy and fill your bucket, too.

A is for Ask

Ask if you can give some help
to your teacher, Mom, or Dad.
You will be so very proud
and they will be so glad.

B is for Be

Be a bucket filler
to your sisters and your brothers,
your classmates and your teachers,
your neighbors and all others.

C is for Cheer

Cheer up a friend who's feeling sad
or someone with a frown.
You can tell a funny joke
or dress up like a clown.

D is for Donate

Donate means to give away
some clothing, food, or toys.
Giving to a special group
helps other girls and boys.

E is for Excited

Excited to fill buckets,
you're a bucketfilling star.
Day and night and always,
no matter where you are.

F is for Friends

Friends will keep your bucket full.
Have fun or just hang out.
To have a friend, be a friend.
That's without a doubt!

G is for Give

Give someone a big, bright smile
or a little of your time.
These are very welcome gifts
that won't cost you a dime.

H is for Heroes

Heroes look out for others.
They are a shining light.
They use their words to speak up
when something isn't right.

I is for Invite

Invite someone who's new
to join in all the fun.
Their bucket will be filled
because of what you've done.

J is for Joyful

Joyful is the feeling
your grandma gives to you.
When you give her a hug,
she's hugging you back, too!

K is for Kindness

Kindness leads to happiness.
It will brighten up your day.
The thoughtful things you say and do
will chase the blues away.

L is for Listen

Listen with your eyes and ears
when other people talk,
while sitting in a classroom
or going for a walk.

is for Make

Make a bucketfilling card.
Write a get-well letter.
Send it to a friend who's sick.
They will feel much better.

N is for Notice

Notice all the helpful things
that other people do.
Tell them that they filled your bucket
and add a big "thank you!"

O is for Offer

Offer your amazing help
when Grandpa has a need.
With your extra pair of hands,
he'll be done in twice the speed.

P is for Practice

Practice is required
for any skill you know.
Fill a bucket every day
and you'll become a pro.

Q is for Quit

Quit any bucket dipping.
It's very mean to do.
Bucket dipping always hurts
and dips your bucket, too.

R is for Respect

Respect is owed to everyone.
It starts when you're polite,
using your good manners,
and treating others right.

S is for Smile

Smile and see what happens.
Does a smile come back to you?
When you fill a bucket,
you are really filling two.

T is for Tell

Tell your family that you love them,
with feelings that are true.
Nothing fills a bucket more
than hearing, "I love you."

U is for Use

Use kind words when you speak.
It hurts when someone dips.
Take the time to stop and think
before you move your lips.

is for Volunteer

Volunteer to do some work,
like tidy up your room.
Do it without being asked
and don't forget the broom!

W is for Watch

Watch out for bucket dipping.
It's a time to use your lid.
It will protect your bucket
from a bucketdipping kid.

X is for eXtra-special

Extra-special is the word
for a bucketfilling friend.
The happiness they bring to you
just never seems to end.

Y is for You

You are a bucket filler.
I'm sure you could have guessed.
You always keep your bucket full
when you do your best.

Z is for Zero

Zero means there's nothing
that you cannot work out
when you are kind to others.
Let's give that a shout!

By now you must have learned this truth:
There will never be an end
to how you can fill buckets
and be a bucketfilling friend.

Be kind and be a bucket filler.
Be careful not to dip.
Use your lid to protect your bucket.
Share these bucketfilling tips!

Carol McCloud, the Bucket Lady, is an early childhood specialist, award-winning author, and popular speaker. As president of Bucket Fillers, Inc. in Brighton, Michigan, she leads a dynamic team of educators who travel the world to create bucketfilling schools, families, workplaces, and communities.

Caryn Butzke is the business manager for Bucket Fillers, Inc. She has worked a combined twenty years in business management, computer information systems, and web design. It's her genuine love for children and her son, Drew, that inspired her to co-author this book, her debut publication.

Glenn Zimmer is a seasoned art director and editorial illustrator. After having worked for more than thirty years in publishing, he began illustrating children's books in 2010. He is a graduate of the Art Institute of Philadelphia and currently serves on the faculty of Moore College of Art and Design in Pennsylvania.

Authors' Acknowledgment:
In the 1960s, Dr. Donald O. Clifton (1924–2003) first created the "Dipper and Bucket" story that has now been passed along for decades. Dr. Clifton later went on to co-author the #1 *New York Times* bestseller *How Full Is Your Bucket?* and was named the Father of Strengths Psychology.

A portion of the proceeds from this book is being donated to Samaritan's Purse to help meet the needs of children and families around the world.

Bucket Filling from A to Z: The Key to Being Happy
By Carol McCloud and Caryn Butzke
Illustrated by Glenn Zimmer
Copyright © 2013, 2017 by Carol McCloud
Originally published in 2013 by Ferne Press
Printed in the United States on recycled paper
Illustrations, cover, and layout design by Glenn Zimmer using colored pencil and watercolor

Summary: From A to Z, children learn bucketfilling tips to be kind and happy.

Library of Congress Cataloging-in-Publication Data
    McCloud, Carol and Butzke, Caryn
    Bucket Filling from A to Z: The Key to Being Happy
    ISBN 978-1-938326-18-9 Hardcover
    ISBN 978-0-9974864-3-8 Paperback
    1. Child development. 2. Bucket filling. 3. Kindness. 4. Happiness. 5. Social skills.
    I. McCloud, Carol and Butzke, Caryn II. Title
    Library of Congress Control Number: 2016918060
    10 9 8 7 6 5 4 3 2

BUCKET FILLOSOPHY® is an imprint of Bucket Fillers, Inc.
PO Box 255, Brighton, MI 48116 • (810) 229-5468
www.bucketfillers101.com